D1383896

WITHDRAWAL

GUYS' GUIDES

Top of Your Game

A Guy's Guide to Looking and Feeling Your Best

Daniel Eshom

the rosen publishing group's
rosen central
New York

For Richard

Published in 2000 by The Rosen Publishing Group, Inc.
29 East 21st Street, New York, NY 10010

First Edition

Cataloging-in-Publication Data

Eshom, Daniel
    Top of your game : a guy's guide to looking and feeling your best / Daniel Eshom.
    p. cm. — (Guys' guides)
    Includes bibliographical references and index.
    Summary: This book for guys includes advice on taking control of one's body through good nutrition and fitness, on respecting one's self, and on taking responsibility for one's behavior and feelings.
    ISBN 0-8239-3083-1
    1. Teenage boys - Health and hygiene - Juvenile literature 2. Teenage boys - Conduct of life - Juvenile literature [1. Boys - Health and hygiene 2. Boys - Conduct of life] I. Title II. Series
    613'.04233 - dc21

Manufactured in the United States of America

<< contents >>

About This Book

It's not easy being a guy these days. You're expected to be buff, studly, and masculine, but at the same time, you're supposed to be sensitive, thoughtful, and un-macho. And that's not all. You have to juggle all of this while you're wading through the shark-infested waters of middle school. So not only are you dealing with raging hormones, cliques, and geeks, and body changes, but you're also supposed to figure out how to be a Good Guy. As if anyone is even sure what that means anyway. It's enough to make you wish for the caveman days, when guys just grunted and wrestled mammoths with their bare hands and stuff.

Being an adolescent is complicated. Take girls, for example. Just five minutes ago—or so it seems—they weren't much different from you and your buddies. Now, suddenly you can't keep your eyes off them, and other parts of your body have taken an interest too. Or maybe you're not interested in girls yet, and you're worried about when you will be. Then there's figuring out where you fit into the middle school world. Are you a jock, a brain, or what? And how come it seems that someone else gets to decide for you? What's up with that?

Yeah, it's tough. Still, you're a smart guy, and you'll figure it all out. That's not to say that we can't all use a hand. That's where this book comes in. It's sort of a cheat sheet for all the big tests that your middle school years throw at you. Use it to help you get through the amazing maze of your life—and to come out alive on the other side.

<<<Excellent News: The Future Is Now>>>

>>Now Entering Guyville. Welcome.<<

OK. Here's the situation . . .

Things are looking up! You've reached the point in your life when things are finally starting to happen. Your body is on the verge of a massive growth and transition period. School is becoming much more challenging. You spend a lot of time wondering about dating, sex, and how exactly you're going to fit into the whole equation. High school is just over the horizon, and college isn't too far behind. Life is getting busier and a lot more interesting . . .

. . . and you know you're ready.

Welcome to Guyville

>>Before You Can Look Your Best, You've Got to Feel Your Best.<<

Sometimes that's easier said than done. Especially when it seems as though the message to guys is not to *feel* things at all. As guys, we're all too often raised to be different from girls. You know all the tired stereotypes: Males are strong-willed and unemotional; females are fickle and hyperemotional.

Whatever.

The fact is, guys have as many emotions and urges as girls. Right now, you're probably experiencing some pretty unfamiliar feelings. Add to this the fact that almost every part of your life is changing at a breakneck pace. On top of puberty and everything else, how can a guy be expected to concentrate on taking care of his body, eating well, and feeling good when he's really feeling kinda stressed, and sorta confused?

If you're feeling slightly helpless, or frustrated about something you think you've failed at, or isolated because you feel different from other boys at school, or freaked out about what's beginning to happen to your body (or worried

First things first (and this isn't your mom giving you lip service):

You're not crazy . . . You're normal!

because nothing's happening to your body yet), or just kind of over- whelmed for reasons you can't quite put your finger on . . . you're simply human. Like

everybody else, you've got a lot to cope with.

So you want to reach the top of your game—the pinna- cle—and stay there. Cool. Start here: The most important tools a boy needs to achieve this goal are self-esteem and self-respect. You've definitely heard these terms before, proba- bly with no concrete advice attached to them. As you read this book, you'll see how self-esteem and self-respect are reflected very clearly in everything you do. Being a guy today is all about having the courage to make your own choices and having the strength to do what's best for you. Trust yourself.

Now let's get to it. No rehearsal. The future is now.

These are strange times to be a preteen or teenage guy. It's no secret that teens rule popular culture. Just turn on the television, go to the movies, or listen to the radio. They're all about perfect-looking teens saving the world from vampires and other assorted evils, falling in and out of highly unlikely comic situations, and singing about their all-consuming love affairs. In magazines, everybody has loads of muscles, expensive clothes, and snow white smiles.

Then reality checks in—because the truth is, you live in the real *Real World*. Naturally, you have a lot of real-world questions. What are the safest, most effective ways to take care of my body during puberty? Which exercises are the best for me? Which foods are good for me, and which should I try to avoid? How do I keep my skin zit-free? Where can I find cool clothes?

Don't look to entertainment media for the answers. Think of it this way: Nine times out of ten, the person responsible for the stuff targeted at your generation is your parents' age. It's important to recognize teen programming and music for what they are: sometimes entertaining, often unrealistic, and definitely not to be taken too seriously.

2

*Your table is ready at **Le Bistro Guy**
Try the special Guy's Guide menu:*

Today's Health Specials*

Plenty-of-Energy Gumbo
marinated in a hearty and invigorating sauce

Maximum Brain Power Stir-Fry
served in a memory-enhancing vinaigrette

Steady-Mood Shish Kebab
slow roasted on an even keel

Good-Looks Gourmet
an excellent presentation, attractive and well arranged

Optimum-Growth Filet
protein-packed and rich with possibility

Sense-of-Control Casserole
with your choice of ingredients

*Cost per item: priceless (plus tax)
Bon appetit, mon frère!

>>Treating Your Body Like a . . . Snowboard?<<

Maybe it strikes you as a little strange to think of your body as a sacred temple. Don't think of it as a temple, then. You might think of it as a sprawling mansion replete with tower-ing marble columns. Or maybe it's a modest but fully stocked condo with a killer view of the mountains. If you like your metaphors a bit more mobile, it could be a high-speed, low-drag, tricked-out Vespa motor scooter. I prefer to think of my body as a smooth-riding, versatile snowboard, carving its way across the mountain that is my life (no laughing).

Ridiculous, right? Doesn't matter, because it works for me. In the end, all that matters is that a guy recognizes his body as his prize possession, something to take care of for the long haul. A famous German philosopher named Friedrich Nietzsche, who apparently knew a thing or two about life, once wrote, "The awakened and knowing say:

Body I am entirely, and nothing else; and soul is only a word for something about the body." Loose translation: The people who really know what's up realize that no matter how you look at life, at the end of the day, it's all about the body.

>>You Are What You Eat. You Eat What You Are.<<

Fact: If you don't feel good, you probably don't look good.

Another fact: If you don't look good, you probably feel worse.

Guys can usually put a finger on what factors cause their moods. Your soccer team loses a big game, and you feel depressed, or you get an A on your math test and feel great. You get the flu and feel like a used Kleenex, or you run a mile through your neighborhood on a sunny

yes!

11

spring morning and feel as though you're practically invincible. You pick on your younger brother—a way-too-easy target—and you feel like a complete jerk, or you do your family's laundry without being asked and suddenly feel that you're on the path to sainthood.

Sometimes, though, a guy can feel sort of blah—tired, apathetic, and down—and be totally clueless about why.

Fact: The food you put into your body directly affects the kind of performance you get out of it, including some of your mysterious mood swings.

Your body is on the verge of the most dramatic and fast-paced growth period of your life: puberty. It might already be happening to you. Now more than ever, nutrition is of the utmost importance. Eat for success. It's the first crucial step toward getting to the top of your game.

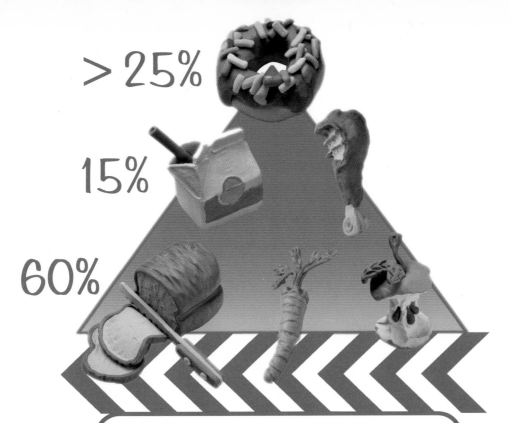

> 25%

15%

60%

Nutrition experts say that the average guy between the ages of eleven and fourteen should try to take in between 2,000 and 3,000 food-and-drink calories per day. Sixty percent of these should come from complex carbohydrates (fruits, vegetables, bread, pasta), about 15 percent from pro-tein (meats, beans, nuts, dairy products), and less than 25 percent from fat (as little saturated fat as possible).

>>Nutrition Basics<<

It really is pretty basic: Your body runs on energy. Energy is measured in terms of calories. Calories are provided by proteins, fats, and carbohydrates. These nutrients, plus vitamins, minerals, and water, make up the diet your body needs to keep going. Period. Food is divided into four basic groups:

- meats and fish
- dairy products
- breads and cereals
- fruits and vegetables

The trick—the part that's not so basic—is figuring out how to balance it all.

>>Food for Thought<<

Snacks high in complex carbohydrates are great for keeping a mental edge. Avoid items high in fat or sugar, which can blunt your sharpness, and try some of these brainy morsels instead....

Fruits: apples, grapes, oranges, pears, cantaloupes, honeydew melons

Vegetables: celery sticks, broccoli, cauliflower, carrots, tomato juice

Whole-grain food: biscuits and rolls, light popcorn, pretzels, whole-wheat toast

The menu from Le Bistro Guy is partly a joke, but it does point out some very serious benefits that are available to the guy who treats his body right. You already know just from plain old common sense how to do this: Don't overeat, lay off sugary and fatty foods, don't smoke or do drugs, and—everybody's favorite—eat your vegetables. But what about the hows and whys behind these rules? Why can't your body thrive on Pop Tarts and Mountain Dew (otherwise known as a strict diet of butter, preservatives, sugar, and caffeine)? If you eat asparagus and broccoli (full of heavy-duty vitamins, minerals, and other nutrients), what's in it for you?

Experts say that the biggest enemies to good nutrition are saturated fat, or excess animal fat, and too much cholesterol. Red meat; certain high-fat dairy products such as whole milk, cheese, and butter; nuts; fried foods; cooking oils; and many salad dressings are all very high in saturated fat. Your body does require a little bit of fat—but a little bit goes a long way.

>>The Buzz on Caffeine<<

Caffeine is a natural product of coffee beans, kola nuts (an ingredient in some soft drinks), tea leaves, and cocoa beans (the main ingredient in

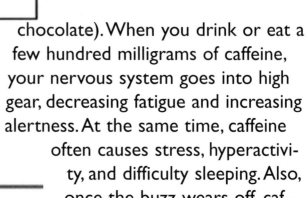

chocolate). When you drink or eat a few hundred milligrams of caffeine, your nervous system goes into high gear, decreasing fatigue and increasing alertness. At the same time, caffeine often causes stress, hyperactivity, and difficulty sleeping. Also, once the buzz wears off, caffeine users usually feel more sluggish and less alert than they did in the first place. It's generally regarded as a drug, and studies have shown that it is addictive, causing withdrawal symptoms such as headaches and irritability. If you drink a lot of caffeinated soda or coffee, remember that they have major diuretic and dehydrating effects, so it's very important to always replenish your body fluids by drinking a good amount of water afterward.

If you want to get beyond the basic building blocks—carbs, protein, and fat—of looking and feeling great, the following table offers a general overview of vitamin and mineral nutrients: what they do for you, and which foods provide them.

>>Sporty Snacks<<

What should you eat before participating in a sports event or exercising? Stay away from potato chips, candy bars, and beef. If you want the real breakfast of champions—or lunch or dinner—nosh on these . . .

low-fiber breads and pastas: energy-feeding and high in carbohydrates

yogurt and skim milk: easy to digest, loaded with calcium and energy

natural fruit juices: lots of vitamins and energy, and they don't weigh you down

Vitamin and Mineral Needs for Growing Guys: A Quick Reference

Vitamins/Minerals	Sources	Benefits
Calcium	dairy products: cheese, milk	bone formation, healthy teeth, healthy nervous system, red blood cell production
Iron	red meat, raisins	red blood cell production
Vitamin A	green/yellow vegetables, carrots, tomatoes	good vision, bone/teeth formation
Vitamin D	fish, egg yolks, fortified milk	healthy heart, healthy nervous system
Vitamin E	eggs, fish, cereals, nuts, vegetables	red blood cell production, healthy heart
Vitamin K	spinach, bran, rice, tomatoes	blood coagulation
Vitamin B1 (Thiamine)	pork, beef, whole grains, beans	healthy nervous system
Vitamin B2 (Riboflavin)	cereals, cheese, milk	red blood cell formation
Vitamin B3 (Niacin)	meat, peanuts, grains	brain function, healthy nervous system
Vitamin B6 (Pyridoxine)	corn, wheat germ, lean meats, bananas	healthy skin, helps reduce cramps
Folic Acid	green leafy vegetables, asparagus, kidney beans	red blood cell formation, healthy heart
Vitamin B12	lean meats, milk, eggs, cheese	promotes growth, improves concentration
Vitamin C	citrus fruits, tomatoes, cabbage, broccoli	heals wounds, helps ward off infection

3

Dear Guy Guide,

Everybody's always sweating me because I don't exercise. What's the big deal? Exercise is too tiring. I never have the energy for it. I have a hard enough time trying to stay alert and make it through my classes. What's wrong with sitting down and watching television after school? I mean, I've gotta rest up so I can do my homework tonight—my grades aren't so hot right now. I wish everybody would just give me a break. I'm in a bad enough mood as it is.

Signed,
Sofa Slug

>>Let's Get Physical<<

We can all totally relate to Sofa Slug. Life is exhausting enough with school, chores, and homework.

Since energy is a guy's most precious commodity, it's a bad idea to waste it on exercise, right?

(You knew this was coming):

Wrong.

Okay, so you're not surprised that a book about how to look and feel your best is going to encourage you to exercise. It's not as if you haven't heard it a million times before. So why is fitness so important for a boy during adolescence?

Consider the case of Sofa Slug. He doesn't have any energy. He has a hard time concentrating at school, and his grades are suffering because of it. He spends his afternoons vegging out in front of the tube. And he sounds pretty grumpy.

Sofa Slug has issues—all of which can be resolved with a regular exercise program. The idea that working out saps your energy is a myth. It may sound weird, but when you expend a lot of energy doing aerobic exercise and working up a sweat, you end up feeling less tired afterward. Exercise gives you more energy. It actually releases chemicals in your body that make you feel good. Do whatever you want—skateboard, dance, jump rope, play frisbee with your dog—but just try it: I guarantee that you'll notice how much better you feel afterwards.

It's not about being a superstar jock. Being really good is not the point. Feeling really good is.

>>Stressed Out About Organized Team Sports?<<

Let's put the all-too-common "I'm not good enough" syndrome in perspective: How many guys can honestly say that they're the best in the school, at the top of the league, the all-around most valuable player? Maybe you're one of them.

Chances are you're not. (Of course, you never know what could happen: Michael Jordan was cut from his high school basketball team.)

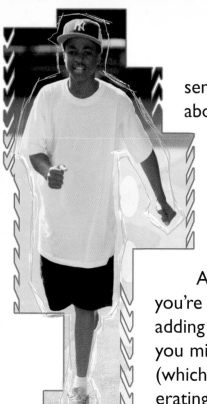

If you're a decent, mediocre, or even semi-bad athlete, it's nothing to feel tragic about. You can deal . . .

A: You're in the overwhelming majority.

B: There are recreational leagues everywhere, in every sport, that emphasize fitness and learning instead of hardcore competition and winning.

And especially C: If you do only the things you're already good at, you could miss out on adding some new tricks to your repertoire, and you might never learn how to laugh at yourself (which is one of life's most indispensable and liberating skills).

Just Do It (Differently).

The Guy's Guide Top Ten List of "Alternative" Sports that Truly Rock:

Capoeira: The ultimate combination of strength, coordination, and precision.

Fencing: Is there another sport with outfits that are this cool?

Juggling: Master three balls, then try four. Then five . . . Work up to flaming batons.

Gymnastics: Springing into the air. Guaranteed muscles. Rad acrobatics. Enough said.

Diving: See above. Add water and sun.

Rock Climbing: All it takes is the body of a triathlete and the mind of a chess wizard.

Tap Dancing: No rules. Just rhythm.

Jai Alai: Just saying the words is fun.

Hackysacking: Mellow, social, and highly addictive.

Kickboxing: Strap on the pads. Commence with the Van Damme-age.

>>If You're Thinking About Taking Anabolic Steroids . . .<<

It's your choice.

So is drinking Drano.

Steroids are illegal for a reason. These drugs do help athletes build more muscle mass, assuming they work out several hours a day while they take them. Steroids also upset the balance of sex hormones, often causing liver problems, impotence, underdeveloped testicles, breast development (yes, in boys), premature baldness, and extreme acne problems. Oh—and a guy's chances of death are seriously increased.

Choose well.

>>How to Be a Bad Sport<<

(Warning: Do not try these at home.)

In a game, if the ref makes a call against you, complain loudly and dramatically.

Construct elaborate, far-fetched excuses about why you made the error.

Never listen to suggestions or strategies from your coach or teammates.

Whenever possible, lace your dialogue with profanities.

Refuse to play unless you get to call all the shots.

If you're losing, quit before it's over.

Hog the ball. Never pass.

Act totally surprised and hurt when friends refuse to play with you anymore.

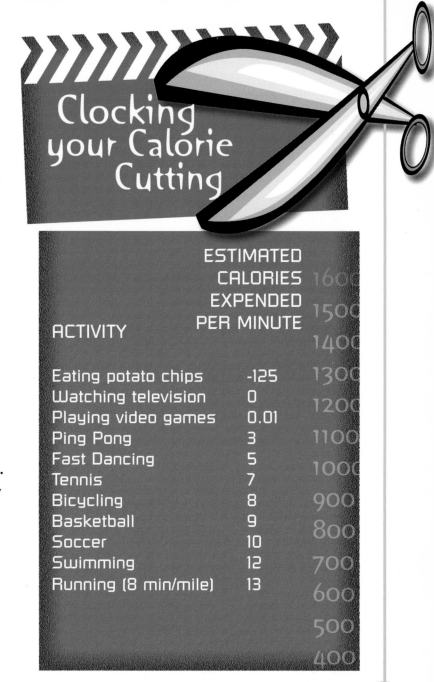

Clocking your Calorie Cutting

ACTIVITY	ESTIMATED CALORIES EXPENDED PER MINUTE
Eating potato chips	-125
Watching television	0
Playing video games	0.01
Ping Pong	3
Fast Dancing	5
Tennis	7
Bicycling	8
Basketball	9
Soccer	10
Swimming	12
Running (8 min/mile)	13

1600
1500
1400
1300
1200
1100
1000
900
800
700
600
500
400

<<<Make a Clean Break: Zits, B.O., and Facial Hair >>>

4

Facial Hair Highway 1 mile ahead

WARNING: B.O. Barricade ahead

>>On the Well-Traveled Road Through Guyville, Everyone Runs into Them Sooner or Later...<<

Pimples. Body odor. Hair sprouting on your face, under your arms, and around your penis.

These are some of the outward signs of puberty, the process of growing up and becoming a man. It's all on schedule. It might already have begun for you—or it might not happen for a couple more years. Everyone develops at his own pace. There is no such thing as too early or too late when it comes to puberty. (If you're really worried about this, it's okay. Ask your dad or mom to take you to the doctor to check things out. It will make you feel better.)

Here's some advice on how to take all of this in stride: As your body changes, it only makes sense that how you groom yourself and keep yourself clean should change as well. The goal is straightforward: You want to be comfortable with your body. You're doing fine.

>>Perspiration and Body Odor<<

At some point, your underarms will begin perspiring more heavily than when you were younger, and your body will give off a different smell than you're used to. Even the palms of your hands might get sweaty occasionally, and you may notice that your genitals and feet also have a different odor. It will probably seem pretty ripe and a little funky to you. You'll know when it happens.

If you lived in another part of the world, most likely you would already be used to it. In many countries, body odor is no big deal. In North America, however, body odor is viewed as something one should avoid at all costs, as if it were a disease. We've all seen the TV commercials encouraging us to get really worked up about staying fresh and dry.

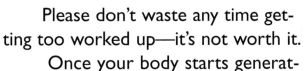

Please don't waste any time getting too worked up—it's not worth it. Once your body starts generating its own B.O., there's absolutely no need to freak. Nothing is wrong with wanting to smell clean and fresh, though. Taking a shower or bath every day—especially after you exercise strenuously—and wearing clean clothes will help. Guys who are heavy-duty perspirers might think about wearing cotton T-shirts under their regular shirts, too.

A lot of guys apply deodorant and/or antiperspirant to their armpits. These odor-fighting products come in sticks, roll-ons, and sprays. Deodorants cover up your body odor with what is supposed to be a more pleasant scent. Most antiperspirants contain a substance called aluminum chlorohydrate to dry up perspiration. Some people believe that the aluminum will soak through your skin, mingle with your bloodstream, and harm you. Others disagree. It's your decision, but no matter what, always read the label.

>>Pimples<<

As your body starts manufacturing hormones during puberty, your skin becomes more oily. For most teenage guys, this extra greasiness leads to skin problems. This doesn't mean that you're dirty. It's more a reflection of what's happening on the inside: Glands beneath your skin start working overtime producing a moisturizing substance called sebum. If a pore gets clogged with too much sebum, a blackhead develops. If it is not removed in time, the blackhead graduates into a full-fledged zit.

>>Tips for Battling Blemishes <<

A few zits never hurt anyone in the long run. Although there are no surefire ways to banish pimples from your domain completely, these steps should help.

- Frequent shampoos will keep greasy, oily hair from mixing with the oil on your skin.

- Wash your face two or three times a day with ordinary soap or a mild antibacterial cleanser. Wash with warm water to open your pores, and rinse with cold to close them again.

- You can buy pads soaked in isopropyl alcohol to wipe away leftover oil and dirt after washing. Be careful, though—these can dry you out.

- If you have zits or blackheads on your shoulders, back, or upper chest, be sure to use an antibacterial soap and a back brush. Never pop blackheads or zits, because then they take longer to heal—and you could wind up with permanent scars or pits.

- Some doctors believe that eating chocolate and salty, fried foods can lead to break-outs. Other doctors disagree. If you notice that your skin problems are triggered by certain foods, then modify your eating habits.

Some guys have to cope with a serious case of infected pimples called acne. Acne is an especially troublesome problem that can lead to severe pitting or scarring of the skin. If you think that you might have acne, you should see a dermatologist, a doctor specializing in skin problems. Among other things, dermatologists can prescribe a drug called tetracycline, which has been very successful in curing acne in some teens.

>>Facial Hair<<

A quick note about total-body hair before we talk about face fuzz . . . Some guys will get really hairy once they hit puberty, sprouting thick hair on their arms, legs, and chest. Some guys will hardly grow any hair, although virtually everyone grows some in the armpits and

around the genitals. Hair growth is caused by a hormone

that your testicles make called testosterone. You might have heard that if a guy doesn't grow much body hair, he has a testosterone deficiency. Don't believe the hype. Testosterone makes your hair grow in the first place, but the amount of body hair you end up with has absolutely nothing to do with the amount of testosterone your testicles churn out. The myth that a guy's masculinity is related to how much chest hair he has is just that—a tired, totally **false myth**.

Usually in the middle or toward the end of the development process, you'll start to grow hair on the lower part of your face and on your neck. It could happen at twelve, or not until you're twenty. For most guys, not much hair grows at first. Facial hair gets thicker and darker over time. Shaving regularly will accelerate this process.

How to Shave

When you first start shaving, you won't need to do it very often—maybe once a week, tops. Don't rush things. Shaving every single day becomes a drag very quickly.

Ask your dad, older brother, or any male adult you feel comfortable with to take you to buy a razor and shaving cream. Ask which products he thinks you should use. There are all kinds. In the beginning, it's probably a good idea to use a basic disposable razor and a cream designed for "sensitive skin." If possible, avoid shaving by yourself the first time.

1. Wet your beard area with medium-hot water. Don't overdo it and scald yourself. Never shave a dry face—you're guaranteed to cut yourself.

2. Apply a thin layer of shaving cream to your upper lip, your chin, and your lower cheeks.

3. Run your razor under hot water for about ten seconds. Make sure your razor is smooth, sharp, and free of nicks. Dull blades can cause cuts and skin irritation.

4. Shave in smooth, downward strokes. Take it slowly. You don't need to press down very hard. Some guys with heavier beards shave in upward strokes, but a lot of guys find that this irritates their skin.

5. Don't shave your whole face! If you're bothered by a "uni-brow"—hair between your eyebrows—dip a pair of tweezers in some rubbing alcohol and pluck the hairs out. It might be a little painful, but it's effective. Never shave between your eyebrows with a razor. The hair will just come back heavier.

6. Rinse with cold water. Some guys put on after-shave lotion to soothe their skin. If you want to try some, look for a product that's alcohol-free (no sting) and either mildly or non-scented.

There's just one more key element to being a good-looking, clean-smelling, hygienic guy: Brush your teeth. Your dentist probably tells you to brush after every meal. If you can't manage that, make sure you do it twice a day—first thing in the morning, last thing at night.

5

>>"Clothes make the man"—Not!<<

The *man* makes the man. But let's be honest: What a guy wears does have an effect on how others see him. More important, his clothes play a part in how he feels about himself.

Style can get tricky. We all know how ferocious school can be for a guy who looks a little different. This is stupid—who wants to be a clone?—but it doesn't make it any less true. Money is a big issue too. Most of us don't have the resources to afford the clothes we'd really like to wear. That's just a fact of life, so it's not worth getting too down about.

>>C'mon, Mom! How Lame!<<

If your parents are pressuring you into wearing clothes that you don't like, there are a few things you can do. Stay calm and explain to them exactly why you don't like their taste in clothes. Show them what you would rather wear. (If what you'd rather wear costs about as much as a new car, forget it. Take a reality pill.) You might even think about writing a brief essay explaining your position. (This could either impress your parents—or really scare them.) If nothing works, and it's important enough to you, set a goal for yourself to earn your own money and buy some of your own clothes.

>>Individual Chic<<

Improvise. Experiment. Keep it real, keep it comfortable, and maybe even find a way to make your look

yeah, right!

reflect your personality. A lot of guys like to shop at secondhand clothing stores, or thrift shops. Vintage and "old-school" clothes are very popular these days. (Added bonus: They're usually a lot less expensive than new clothes.)

Some guys like to wear close-fitting pants and tight shirts. This style can look good on the right person, but what if you're in the midst of a major growth spurt with no end in sight? The tighter the clothes, the faster you'll outgrow them. You might want to wait a few years before you start going for the sleek look. In fact, it's not a bad idea to buy your clothes a little big so that they last longer. Most guys wear baggy clothes because they find them more comfortable.

>>Fashion 101<<

Unless you want to work a look that inspires comparisons to a car crash (and if that's your thing, right on—try it out), you probably want your clothes to match. This is an acquired skill, but it's not rocket science. Despite what some people and magazines might tell you, there are no absolute fashion dos or don'ts. However, it doesn't hurt to keep some basic tips in mind:

> Blue jeans are "neutral": It's safe to wear them with almost any color shirt or sweater.

> Don't mix patterned/striped/plaid shirts with patterned/striped/plaid pants. (Someone might mistake you for a golfer.)

> Go with your instincts: If you have a hunch that your purple T-shirt clashes with those orange shorts, trust yourself. (Please trust yourself.)

> A thin guy who wants to look a little bigger can try wearing shirts with horizontal stripes.

> Bigger guys often look good in vertical stripes.

> If the label says "100% cotton," buy a bigger size than you need—it will shrink when you wash it.

> Wool is itchy. Make sure that you can deal.

> Always try stuff on before buying! If you're buying something over the phone from a catalog, find out about the company's return and exchange policies first.

>>Big Hair, Big Dreams . . . The Scalp Scoop<<

Whether you wear your hair long, medium, or very short, it's a good idea to get it cut or trimmed every four to five weeks. The ends of your hairs get damaged and frayed after a while, so you shouldn't let it go too long between cuts. There are lots of barbers and salons who will do a good job for not much money. Look in the phone book.

If you want to have more control over your hair, there are all kinds of gels, mousses, and sprays you can choose from at the store. They're not just for girls. As always, read the label. If you try one, remember that a little bit goes a long way. Don't go too wet-look crazy.

To avoid damaging and pulling out some of your hair, try not to brush it when it's wet—that's when it's weakest.

If your hair tends to be dry—rather than oily—avoid using a blow dryer. Letting it dry naturally works fine.

To avoid turning your hair into straw, always shampoo and condition after swimming in salt water or chlorinated pools.

Got a bad haircut? No worries. It will grow out in a month or two.

Style means a lot more than just your hairstyle and the clothes you wear. Your style is reflected in the way you act, how you feel, and the way you treat your friends and family. Granted, wearing clothes with that you're comfortable with definitely makes you look good, which automatically makes you feel good. And that's the whole reason you're reading this book, right? Just try not to get too hung up on clothing. (Then again, if you're planning to go into fashion design when you're older, that's another story. Go to it. Get hung up on clothing all you want!)

In the end, finding your own style is part of a much bigger, more important, and far more exciting journey—a journey that will continue throughout your life. It's called getting to know yourself.

>>Grace Under Pressure<<

Things can get overwhelming and even intimidating these days. But a lot of guys like you are going through the same stuff—and keeping their cool. Check out what these guys have to say about handling stress, destroying stereotypes, and coping with peer pressure.

At first I was psyched to start middle school, you know? But everything changed fast. The guys from my old homeroom who I used to hang out with suddenly started acting all 'cool' and tough. A couple of them started smoking. They were totally different than when they were in elementary school. I thought if I didn't start acting the same way, they'd make fun of me. It's a big school, though, and I've made other friends.
—Jack, 13

There are things that boys are supposed to do—play sports, get girls, try to find ways to get beer. But guess what? Some of us just aren't like that. Some of us are into drawing comics, programming computers, writing new-school funk music, volunteering, even cooking. I write short stories. Whatever a guy does should be respected.
—Tyson, 11

>>Knowledge Equals Power. Power Up.<<

Although it can be tough, life is also becoming very exciting: You're growing up, and the whole world, with its infinite possibilities, is finally opening up to you. Feel free to ask questions of your teachers, your parents, your doctor, or any other adult you trust. Go to the Web sites listed in It's a Guy's World. Read the great books recommended in the Get Booked section. The more you know, the better. Exercise your rights. (See following page.)

Life is happening to you right now.

Enjoy the ride.

The Guy's Guide Bill of Rights

Sometimes life can feel like a giant pressure cooker. It seems as if there are all sorts of unwritten rules and codes for how a guy is supposed to act. Who makes these rules up? It's a mystery.

Only two rules matter: Respect yourself. Be yourself.

Easy to say. Much harder to do, right? Maybe this will help.

- To be treated with respect, no matter who you are.

- To take responsibility for your behavior, your thoughts, and your feelings.

- To take control of your body and mood through good nutrition and smart fitness.

- To feel proud of your own opinions, interests, and passions.

- To ask questions when you're curious or confused about something.

- To be the person you want to be—and to like that person.

aerobic exercise Any type of steady total-body movement in
which breathing keeps up with the body's increased oxygen
requirements. A great way to condition the heart and lungs and
improve blood circulation. Also called cardiovascular (heart and
blood vessels) exercise, or cardiopulmonary (heart and lungs)
exercise.

anabolic steroids A synthetic, or man-made, hormone used to
increase muscle size and strength unnaturally.

blemishes Pimples, zits, and other flaws appearing on the skin.

caffeine A chemical compound found in coffee, tea, and kola nuts
and used as a stimulant and diuretic.

carbohydrates A large group of chemical compounds found in
food. Complex carbohydrates include fruit, vegetables, and cereal
grains. Simple carbohydrates include sugar, soda, cookies, and
other junk foods.

cholesterol A substance in the bloodstream caused by the
intake of animal fats found in butter, eggs, and meat. A high
level of cholesterol can cause clogged arteries and heart disease.

diuretic A substance that causes a loss of body water through
increased urination.

hormone   A biological messenger created by human glands and sent through the bloodstream to affect other parts of the body. Examples include growth hormones, sex hormones, and insulin.

media   Newspapers, magazines, television, radio, and other types of communication that reach large numbers of people.

protein   The substance in food that gives the body energy and works to build muscles, hormones, and other essential elements.

puberty   The stage during which boys' and girls' bodies begin to take on adult characteristics and become physically able to reproduce, or produce babies.

sebum   An oily substance produced by glands in the skin. During puberty the body may produce extra sebum, which often leads to skin blemishes.

stereotype   A conventional, oversimplified, and usually inaccurate opinion or belief about something.

testosterone   A male sex hormone produced in the testicles that controls pubic and sexual development.

<<< It's a Guy's World >>>

Web Sites

Fitness Link
http://www.fitnesslink.com/changes/kidsfit.htm

The Food Zone
http://kauai.cudenver.edu:3010/

KidsHealth.org
http://www.kidshealth.org/teen/

National Clearinghouse for Alcohol and Drug
   Information for Kids Only
http://www.health.org/kidsarea/

React.com (on-line zine)
http://www.react.com

Ten Tips to Healthy Eating and Physical Activity
http://ificinfo.health.org/10tipkid.htm

Virtual Kid's Puberty 101
http://www.virtualkid.com/p101_menu.html

44

<<< Get Booked >>>

Blume, Judy. *Then Again, Maybe I Won't.* New York: Laurel Leaf, 1976.

Chbosky, Stephen. *The Perks of Being a Wallflower.* New York: Pocket Books, 1999.

Konigsburg, E.L. *The View from Saturday.* New York: Aladdin Paperbacks, 1998.

Madaras, Lynda, and Dane Saavedra. *The What's Happening to My Body? Book for Boys.* New York: Newmarket Press, 1988.

McCoy, Kathy, and Charles Wibbelsman. *Life Happens: A Guide to Friends, Failure, Sexuality, Love, Rejection, Addiction, Peer Pressure, Families, Loss, Depression, Change, and Other Challenges of Living.* New York: Putnam Berkley, 1996.

Palmer, Pat, and Melissa A. Froehner. *Teen Esteem: A Self-Direction Manual for Young Adults.* San Luis Obispo, CA: Impact Publishers, 1989.

Roehm, Michelle, ed. *Boys Know It All: Wise Thoughts and Wacky Ideas from Guys Like You.* Hillsboro, OR: Beyond Words Publishing, 1998.

Salter, Charles A. *Food Risks and Controversies: Minimizing the Dangers in Your Diet (A Teen Nutrition Book).* Brookfield, CT: Millbrook Press, 1993.

<<< Index >>>

<<< Credits >>>

About the Author

Daniel Eshom is a writer, editor, and middle-school survivor. He lives in New York City.

Photo Credits

Cover photo © Artville; p. 21 © Cheryl Maeder/FPG; p. 23 © Agency Vandystadt; p. 24 © CORBIS. All other photographs by Thaddeus Harden.

Series Design

Oliver H. Rosenberg

Layout

Laura Murawski